100

THINGS TO DO IN
CHARLOTTE
BEFORE YOU
DIE

100

THINGS TO DO IN
CHARLOTTE
BEFORE YOU
DIE

●●●●●●●●●●●●●●●●●●●●●●●●●●●

SARAH CROSLAND

REEDY PRESS

Reedy Press
PO Box 5131
St. Louis, MO 63139, USA
www.reedypress.com

Library of Congress Control Number: 2014946133

ISBN: 9781935806820

Design by Jill Halpin

Printed in the United States of America
16 17 18   5 4 3 2

Please note that websites, phone numbers, addresses, and company names are subject to change or cancellation. We did our best to relay the most accurate information available, but due to circumstances beyond our control, please do not hold us liable for misinformation. When exploring new destinations, please do your homework before you go.

CONTENTS

PREFACE

OK, so the title may sound a little ominous, but don't let that deter you. This is a bucket list of the best kind. There are no rules to when and how these things get checked off, and—hopefully—the deadline is a long, long way away.

I've been covering these kinds of activities as a lifestyle writer in Charlotte since 2008 (tough job, huh?), but even with that much time in a profession dedicated to finding the city's best offerings, I still occasionally find myself on a Saturday afternoon wondering what to do around town.

Enter this book. Coming up with one hundred things wasn't hard. It was narrowing it down to one hundred that was difficult. Turns out, Charlotte is brimming with innovative attractions, unusual experiences, and just plain fun stuff.

So consider this your guide to discovering the things you might not know about—and remembering to do those things you keep saying you want to try. (Yes, the Mint Museum really is worth a visit. And it's true, Central Avenue does have some of the best ethnic fare around. And wouldn't a Sunday biking the Greenway be so much more fun than another one on the couch?)

• •

I'd suggest trying all these things. Maybe, though, for your wallet's sake, not in a hurry. Helicopter rides, NFL games, and concerts can get a little pricey, but jump in and indulge in a few. Hop around and check them off as you go, or check out the Suggested Itineraries in the back of the book if order is your thing. Also be sure to join other readers on Facebook (100ThingsCLT) to report on what you discover. I'd love to hear what else would be on *your* list!

Sarah Crosland

100
THINGS TO DO IN
CHARLOTTE
BEFORE YOU
DIE

FOOD AND DRINK

SAY CHEERS WITH BEERS ON TUESDAYS
AT NODA BREWING

Sure, you could stop by this craft brewery's hopping North Tryon Street taproom anytime for one of their beloved brews, such as the Ramble on Red ale or the award-winning Coco Loco porter, but you'll want to mark off at least one Tuesday on your calendar. Head Brewer Chad Henderson gets creative each week with a new "Nodable" beer tapped on Tuesdays at 4 P.M. Past favorites have included brews like Thrilla' in Vanilla, an American brown ale packed with vanilla beans, and Ghost Hop, an IPA infused with potent ghost peppers. But these tiny-batch brews are only available in the taproom, and they go fast, so order up a pint—or two—to sip and sample.

2921 N. Tryon St., 704-900-6851
nodabrewing.com

Charlotte's microbrewery scene just keeps growing. Want to hit others for a taste of the city's latest craft? Here are a few top spots:

The Olde Mecklenburg Brewery

A family-friendly restaurant, sunny beer garden, and flavorful lineup of German-inspired brews make this South End spot a favorite.

4150 Yancey Rd., 704-525-5644
oldemeckbrew.com

Heist Brewery

Small-batch beers with Monday releases, tasty fare, beer cocktails by a talented mixologist, and a lively taproom draw crowds to this NoDa spot.

2909 N. Davidson St., 704-375-8260
heistbrewery.com

Birdsong Brewing Company

Located just down the street from the original NoDa Brewing, this casual brewery's cozy taproom and spicy brews (try the MexiCali Stout or the Jalapeno Pale Ale) make it a top spot for local beer lovers.

2315 N. Davidson St., 704-332-1810
birdsongbrewing.com

CHOW DOWN
AT PRICE'S CHICKEN COOP

Bring cash . . . and a serious appetite. Maybe Wet-Naps too. At this famed fried chicken joint in South End, you should throw out the diet plan and throw in an extra order of hush puppies. This tiny, family-run spot features a walk-up-and-order counter offering the juiciest and most tender fried chicken in town. They only accept cash, and if you're not drinking the syrupy sweet tea, there's a vending machine for drinks because the crispy chicken is the focus. There's no seating, which means you could take this to go (and likely eat it before you even put the car in drive), but for the real Price's experience, find a spot in the grass across the street and enjoy the city's favorite comfort food in the warmth of the sun.

1614 Camden Rd., 704-333-9866
priceschickencoop.com

TOAST TO THE TOWN
AT THE PUNCH ROOM

Prefer to imbibe above street level? At Uptown's Ritz-Carlton, those in search of a sip can always indulge in the luxe lobby lounge, but it's the hotel's fifteenth floor lounge, The Punch Room, that steals the show. This glamorous drinking den with gold accents and skyline views features some of the city's best cocktails by master mixologist Bob Peters. The Gatsby-like experience includes boozy punches and innovative cocktails, all set to sip by candlelight. Classics with a twist, like the Carbonated Aviation, are the perfect way to kick off or wind down an evening Uptown.

201 E. Trade St., 704-547-2244
ritzcarlton.com

TIP

The Ritz-Carlton is a LEED Gold–certified hotel with two rooftop beehives. The cocktail menu here frequently features buzzy beverages made with the rooftop honey. It's worth checking with your server to see if any seasonal offerings include the sweet treat.

INDULGE IN AMELIE'S SALTED CARAMEL BROWNIES
IN THE MIDDLE OF THE NIGHT

You could always pop into Amelie's French Bakery for hot coffee and a fresh croissant with the prework crowd. Or, you could settle in at this Parisian-inspired eclectic NoDa café for a soup and sandwich lunch. You certainly wouldn't go wrong by coming by for a colorful macaroon dessert, with such flavors as pistachio and raspberry, but this is Charlotte's only twenty-four-hour restaurant, and its after-hours crowd is one of its most charming features. For the perfect late-night snack, try the bakery's famed salted caramel brownies—they're rich bites of chocolate topped in a thick caramel with a slightly salty edge. You'll want to share games and conversation with friends around one of the quaint café tables, but you definitely won't want to share the brownies.

2424 N. Davidson St., Ste. 102, 704-376-1781
ameliesfrenchbakery.com

GET GROOVY OVER BRUNCH
AT SOUL GASTROLOUNGE

On the second Sunday of each month, this hip Plaza Midwood restaurant renders every other brunch in town boring. Its popular disco and drag queen brunch packs the house with a live DJ rocking funky beats as a sequin-adorned drag queen takes the floor to dance around the small space. Need a little more spice in your morning? Start with one of the Absolut Pepper Bloody Marys. And the menu completes the out-of-the-box brunch experience with such dishes as scrambled egg–stuffed pierogies paired with maple syrup–glazed cubes of fried bologna or omelet fettuccine carbonara made with egg strips tossed with smoked salmon in a carbonara sauce. Hungry yet? Brunch starts at 11 A.M. and get there early because this '70s-era eating experience fills up fast.

1500 Central Ave., 704-348-1848
soulgastrolounge.com

EAT AL FRESCO
IN ROMARE BEARDEN PARK

Pleasant park benches near waterfalls and green space? Check. Stunning skyline views? Check. Nearby food trucks and takeout? Check. It would be hard to find a better spot in Uptown to dine on a warm day than in this picturesque park on the west side of the city. Since its opening in the fall of 2013, this grassy spot with scenic views has been a fast favorite for Uptown dwellers and workers, and if you're looking for a spot to soak in the city scene before a Knights baseball game at the adjacent BB&T Ballpark, this is as good as it gets. So grab a bite from one of the local food trucks that often park near the space, and enjoy some of the best dining seats in town.

300 S. Church St., 704-432-4280
charmeck.org

FEAST ON LOCAL FARE
AT 7TH STREET PUBLIC MARKET

Packed with artisanal culinary booths and local purveyors, this is Charlotte's answer to famed city markets, like Philly's Reading Terminal or London's Borough. While our version may not have quite the selection (yet), the bustling dining area is filled with food lovers ordering up offerings ranging from locally sourced chorizo pizzas to fresh-baked bread sandwiches. In the back section of the market, creative chefs can find such items as international spices, North Carolina cheeses, locally grown vegetables, and farm-to-fork meats. The best time to pop in for a bite, though, may be in the morning when vendor Not Just Coffee serves up its steaming mugs of pour-over coffees, which pair perfectly with one of the fresh-baked baguettes or biscuits across the market at Local Loaf.

224 E. Seventh St.
7thstreetpublicmarket.com

DIG INTO
FOOD TRUCK FARE
IN SOUTH END AND PLAZA MIDWOOD

It would be hard to find a food event as beloved in Charlotte as Food Truck Fridays. The city's top trucks first gathered at an empty lot in South End. But starting in the spring of 2016, the trucks are pulling in at the popular Sycamore Brewery in South End and at the parking lot for the Light Factory in Plaza Midwood. Both neighborhood locations are close to plenty of other spots to mix, mingle, or grab a drink after indulging in your food truck fare. And plan on doing some serious indulging. In addition to entrees from such trucks as the Tin Kitchen and Papi Queso, hungry attendees can choose from various sweets at mobile bakeries, including Southern Cake Queen. Plan on waiting in line and likely sitting in the grass—but that's half the fun at these family-friendly evenings.

Sycamore Brewing, 2161 Hawkins St., 704-910-3821
The Light Factory, 1817 Central Ave., 704-333-9755
Foodtruckfridaycharlotte.com

HOP ABOARD
CHARLOTTE BREW TOURS

Charlotte's beer scene is hopping! Want a taste? Sign up for a Saturday brew tour. The tours begin at 1:15 on Saturday afternoons and hit a variety of area breweries, with pints offered at each stop until the tour ends at 6 P.M. While the breweries vary depending on the day, participants typically have the chance to hit at least four of the local spots in the NoDa and South End neighborhoods. Head brewers and owners often offer the tours, which means you'll get an up-close and behind-the-scenes look at the brewing process. These breweries also offer some seriously tasty premium craft beer, so whether you're a beer novice or brew expert, you'll find a pint to toast on this trip.

Pick up at 2226 N. Davidson St.
cltbrewtours.com

PREPARE AND PARTAKE
AT BAR COCOA

Cooking with class is easy when you're taking your instructions in the pristine kitchen of Uptown's Ritz-Carlton hotel. The hotel's Bar Cocoa, a chocolate-centric dessert bar full of sweet delicacies, features weekly Cocoa Lab classes in its state-of-the-art teaching kitchen. With a limited class size of eight participants, these are intimate lessons straight from the pastry chef. Whether you're an amateur in your own kitchen or a hopeful chef, the classes come with plenty of tips (i.e., how to store your vanilla beans or how to best measure flour). Best of all, however, is that the classes come with the chance to indulge in final products, such as chocolate eclairs, hand-rolled truffles, crème brûlée, or strawberry shortcake. Be sure to take your recipe packet when you leave. You're going to want to re-create these decadent desserts in your own kitchen.

201 E. Trade St., 704-972-4397, barcocoacharlotte.com

TIP

For a fun splurge or special occasion, take the Chocolate and Champagne Lovers Workshop. The class, which includes three desserts paired with champagne, is especially decadent—and fun. Add a glass of Dom Perignon for an additional $40, and toast your sweet new skills.

MIX IT UP
AT EARL'S GROCERY

Charlotte is awash in cocktail bars crafting creative—and potent—drinks. For the ultimate local libation experience, head to the Mixology Lab at Earl's Grocery in Elizabeth. These free classes are led by the enthusiastic Bob Peters, who is more mad scientist than mixologist. Before you start crafting elixirs, grab a bite from Earl's tasty lunch menu featuring locally-sourced dishes often with an Asian twist such as banh mi or ramen. Then, head to the front of the charming shop where Peters lines up his liquors at tables alongside the tall windows and offers entertaining demonstrations. You'll have the chance to learn how he shakes, smokes, stirs, shaves, and squeezes to turn each cocktail into a potent masterpiece almost too pretty to drink—almost.

1609 Elizabeth Ave., 704-333-2757,
earlsgrocery.com

GET SCHOOLED IN SCOTCH
AT BALLANTYNE RESORT

Take a sip of your favorite single malt at the Gallery Bar at Ballantyne Resort in South Charlotte. This sophisticated bar featuring wood paneling and golf course views offers the state's largest collection of single malt Scotch whisky—and a Scotch Society with tastings and the chance to learn more about the spirit's rich history. Held on the last Friday of each month, the twenty-person gatherings include complementary dishes and three to four different Scotch offerings for $40. Sign up early to sample and socialize, as these events almost always sell out. Of course, if you can't make the event, the bar itself always offers an impressive selection of Scotch and is the perfect spot to start an evening at Gallery Restaurant, one of Charlotte's top dining destinations.

10000 Ballantyne Commons Pkwy., 704-248-4100
gallery-restaurant.com

TAP INTO KOMBUCHA
AT LENNY BOY BREWERY

If you haven't tried this trendy, effervescent tea yet, you're in luck. There's no place better to take your first sip than at the Lenny Boy Brewery's South End taproom. Here, you can order the organic, fermented drink in flavors like sweet potato, beet, and ginger. In addition to the nonalcoholic versions of the probiotic drink, the brewery also offers its wild ales. These kombucha beers are gluten free and created in the same microbrewery. Take home a growler filled with the Lost Rose made with calming herbs and rose petals or the Mint Condition brewed with spearmint and peppermint. Or, settle in for a pint of one of their beers in the casual and cozy taproom, where you're likely to find the friendly owner—and occasionally even his dog, Lenny.

2224 Hawkins St., 704-458-3202
discoverlennyboy.com

BIKE FOR BEERS AND BBQ
AT MAC'S

Just driving past Mac's Speedshop on a warm, sunny day is almost impossible. Crowds pack the biker bar's outdoor picnic tables, where you'll often find live music, and you'll always find great barbecue and brews. The original South End location, formerly a transmission shop and car wash, has become a favorite for visiting celebrity chefs, including Mario Batali and Anthony Bourdain. And with good reason. The menu here features pulled pork sandwiches so big you'll need two hands, and smoked beef brisket that could compete with any this side of Texas. An extensive beer list includes craft brews from around the country, but it's the laid-back vibe that really draws the crowds. The five friends who launched this barbecue joint loved riding motorcycles, and the best way to hit Mac's is still on the back of a bike.

2511 South Blvd., 704-522-6227
macspeedshop.com

DINE EXPERIENTIALLY
WITH RELISH SUPPER CLUB

Bring your plate. Mingle for a moment. Sit down. Chat with the stranger next to you. Dig in to creative chef-prepared— albeit often simple—food and drink. Share a laugh with that stranger. Indulge a little more in the fare, and suddenly they're not a stranger anymore. That's the idea behind Relish Carolina's exquisite dining events. The group, which hosts several events annually, was founded on the premise that great ideas and innovation begin around a dinner table—and these are some serious dinner tables. From a farm-to-fork event in a local market to a paella dinner paired with sweet sangrias to a beer-and-cheese-focused dinner inside a brewery, the group creates unforgettable evenings for its guests. All you have to do is buy your ticket, bring your own plate, and introduce yourself to your companions for the evening.

relishcarolina.org

WALK THIS WAY
WITH FEAST FOOD TOURS

Whether you're a newbie to the city's restaurant world or just hoping for a behind-the-scenes look into some of your favorite chefs' kitchens, this local culinary tour company will have you licking your lips. The walking tours include neighborhoods like NoDa and Plaza Midwood as well as Uptown. The best one to kick off your culinary adventure is the Soul of the South Tour. For $49, you'll have the chance to sip and sample Southern cuisine around Uptown. While the tour is focused on the soul food side, Southern also means bites at the local market from nearby farmers and artisans and sips of craft beers from local breweries. The tour destinations vary depending on the date, but on each walk you'll have the chance to glimpse Old South architecture as the perfect side dish to your day of dining.

980-258-9992
feastfoodtours.com

CHOP UP YOUR COOKING ROUTINE
AT ATHERTON MARKET

Ready to slice and dice (and bake and boil) your way to a fresh, seasonally sourced meal? Sign up for one of Chef Alyssa's cooking classes held in South End's charming Atherton Market. The classes, which are offered in five different levels based on your culinary prowess, are designed around products available in the respective season. In the summer, you'll find dishes featuring juicy tomatoes and berries, while colder weather offers classes on cozier options, like sweet potato soup or roasted beet salad. And half the fun of the class is its bubbly and extremely knowledgeable leader, Alyssa Gorelick. The young chef with an extensive restaurant background in upscale fare assists in hands-on demos and offers insight into local farms and culinary techniques for healthy fare.

2104 South Blvd., 704-817-7568
chefalyssaskitchen.com

GRAB A SLICE
AT THE ORIGINAL FUEL PIZZA

These days folks in New York City and Washington, D.C., can get in on their slice of the Fuel pie with new locations in both cities, but the original location of the casual pizza joint is right here in Charlotte in the heart of Plaza Midwood at, of course, a former gas station. Launched in 1988 by New Yorkers craving great pizza in Charlotte, the original location still holds its laid-back charm. Order up a hot slice with the famed homemade sauce, grab one of the cold cans of PBR, and settle in at one of the sidewalk picnic tables for the authentic Fuel experience.

1501 Central Ave., 704-376-3835
fuelpizza.com

STAR-STALK
AT 5CHURCH

Hoping to catch a glimpse of whatever musical star has stopped in town on tour? Or maybe see a homegrown celebrity like *The Bachelorette*'s Emily Maynard or the Carolina Panthers' Cam Newton? This swanky Uptown restaurant is the place to do it. Some of its most notable celeb snagging came during the Democratic National Convention in 2012, when Jessica Alba, Elizabeth Banks, and Zach Braff all indulged in the fashionable fare. The trendy traffic hasn't slowed, though, with performers and Hollywood names often making this a stop on their way through town. So grab a seat at the bustling bar, order one of the signature cocktails, and keep an eye out for familiar faces.

127 N. Tryon St., 704-919-1322
5church.com

WARM UP
AT LUPIE'S CAFÉ

When it comes to cozying up on a cold night, this casual landmark restaurant on Monroe Road is the perfect spot. The brick building with its weathered sign and unexpected location doesn't look like much from the outside, but don't be deterred. With walls covered in black-and-white photos of local landmarks and a menu focused on varieties of simmering chili, this down-home spot is ideal for a relaxed evening meal. The sweet and spicy Cincinnati chili topped with onions and cheese is their hearty trademark. Pair it with a slice of hot cornbread and cool sweet tea in a mason jar for the ultimate homey evening.

2718 Monroe Rd., 704-374-1232
lupiescafe.com

TAKE AN INTERNATIONAL FOOD VOYAGE
DOWN CENTRAL AVENUE

Craving Caribbean? In the mood for Mexican? Feel like pho? The multicultural, ethnically diverse Central Avenue to the east of Charlotte is the answer to all of your international food desires. At Mama's Caribbean Grill, you can listen to reggae music while you chow down on Jamaican jerk chicken or goat curry. Just down the road, order up a plate of enchiladas poblanas at Three Amigos while you catch the latest Mexican soccer match. Farther down the street, you'll find Dim Sum, Charlotte's pork-bun-and-steamed-dumplings answer to bigger cities' Chinatown restaurants. Beyond that is Ben Thanh, a family-owned Vietnamese restaurant offering steaming bowls of fresh pho. And interspersed among all of these are small restaurants, markets, and shops offering even more tasty global fare. Hungry yet? Get packing.

Mama's Caribbean Grill
1504 Central Ave., 704-375-8414
mamacaribbeangrill.webs.com

Three Amigos
2917 Central Ave., 704-536-1851
threeamigoscharlotte.com

Dim Sum Chinese Restaurant
2920 Central Ave., 704-569-1128
dimsumcharlotte.com

Ben Thanh
4900 Central Ave., 704-566-1088
benthanhcharlotte.com

CELEBRATE A SPECIAL OCCASION
AT THE MCNINCH HOUSE

This formal restaurant set in a historic Victorian home in Fourth Ward isn't the kind of spot you casually drop by. Upon arrival guests are greeted so warmly it feels as if you're entering someone's private home. (This was formerly the home of Mayor Sam McNinch who once hosted President William Howard Taft in it on his visit to Charlotte in 1909.) McNinch's lavish and hushed rooms offer classical music and candlelight dining on fine china that matches the elegant nature of the fixed-price, French-influenced menu. Such elaborate dishes as foie gras, spiced duck breast, and wild salmon pair well with wines from the restaurant's award-winning list. And for the final, slightly-over-the-top touch? Women are given a long-stemmed and fragrant red rose as they depart the inherently romantic home.

511 N. Church St., 704-332-6159
mcninchhouserestaurant.com

INDULGE IN ICE CREAM
AT PIKE'S SODA SHOP

Sure, you could soak in the sun on Pike's trolley track–side patio or slide into one of the booths in its vintage-inspired dining area with décor from bygone days. But for the real old-timey experience at this South End soda shop and diner, you'll want to pull up a stool at its colorful soda fountain and order a freshly made creamy float, malt, or even banana split. Between the old-fashioned pharmacy tile walls and 1950s tunes playing in the background, this classic spot inspires nostalgia—and likely a craving for one of its IBC root beer floats.

1930 Camden Rd., 704-372-0092
pikessodashop.com

PULL IN
AT BAR-B-Q KING

This West Charlotte barbecue joint has been serving up its famed barbecue fried chicken, po'boys, and chopped pork sandwiches for more than fifty years. Not that this will come as a surprise when you see the place with its red curbside service sign and retro design. Visits from the Food Network's *Diners, Drive-ins & Dives* and *The Best Thing I Ever Ate* have drawn national attention to this small, casual spot for its incredibly tasty—and messy—barbecue chicken. For a seriously Southern meal, order it with the coleslaw and hush puppies, and wash it all down with a cold cherry lemon Sun Drop.

2900 Wilkinson Blvd., 704-399-8344
barbqking.com

DRINK AND DON'T DRIVE
ON THE LIGHT RAIL

There are future plans to extend Charlotte's light rail system, but for now the LYNX light rail features one route from South Charlotte into Center City. Luckily, that route takes you by several top watering holes—perfect for visiting when you've left your car at home. Make your first stop at New Bern and walk up the block to Good Bottle Company for a few craft beers from the frequently rotating taps. From there, head over to Triple C Brewing Company and order up a pint of the Light Rail Pale Ale featuring a citrus kick. Further up the line from the Bland Street station, pop in to Stache House Bar & Lounge for cocktails and nightly drink specials. Of course, once you've made it into Center City, there's no shortage of bars, restaurants, and nightclubs serving up liquid libations. Looking for the easiest option? The CTA/Arena stop spits you out at the city's ultimate nighttime entertainment destination, EpiCentre.

Good Bottle Co.
125 Remount Rd., 704-527-1003
goodbottleco.com

Triple C Brewing Company
2900 Griffith St., 704-372-3212
triplecbrewing.com

Stache House Bar & Lounge
1520 South Blvd., 980-335-0530
stachehouseclt.com

EpiCentre
201 E. Trade St., 704-688-5980
epicentrenc.com

MUSIC AND ENTERTAINMENT

SING THE BLUES
AT BLUE

Go on a Wednesday through Saturday night. Order the classic martini (the restaurant offers an extensive list of signature versions) and one of the Mediterranean appetizers—the crispy risotto balls stuffed with pancetta and sweet onions are great! Then settle in at the sleek bar for live jazz music from local trios and bands. Located on the bottom floor of Uptown's Hearst Tower, this swank restaurant has long been a favorite for those who enjoy urbane fare with a side of jazzy tunes. Its sophisticated setting featuring bronze accents and candlelight sets the tone for the rich tunes, and its central location means that this is often a pre- or postperformance destination for nights at the Blumenthal Performing Arts Center or Time Warner Cable Arena. The best way to experience this spot—and its music—is to linger for the evening with your cocktail as you soak in the sounds.

206 N. College St., 704-927-2583
bluecharlotte.com

SOAK IN THE SCENE
AT FESTIVAL IN THE PARK

There's nothing that says good, old-fashioned family fun like an outdoor fall festival. Charlotte's largest and longest running, Festival in the Park, packs more than eighty-five thousand people into Freedom Park each September. At this Friday through Sunday extravaganza, you can take in the tunes of performers on the main stage, shop the booths brimming with local art, or bite into barbecue or burgers from a Charlotte restaurant. With hundreds of vendors and performers, there are plenty of ways to immerse yourself in Charlotte's craftiest weekend. Can't get enough culture? Lights around the park's lake means this fest lasts into the evening, making it a perfect stop for dinner and browsing.

1409 East Blvd., 704-338-1060
festivalinthepark.org

TAP ALONG TO JAZZ TUNES
AT THE BECHTLER MUSEUM OF MODERN ART

On the first Friday of each month, Uptown's modern art mecca fills with jazz-loving concertgoers for its performances by the Ziad Jazz Quartet. Each evening includes two full shows (6 to 7:30 P.M. and 8:15 to 9:45 P.M.) that typically sell out. Grab a glass of wine and an appetizer from the museum's cash bar before the show, and then soak in the swinging sounds in the museum's soaring atrium—within view of the museum's brightly colored Andy Warhol paintings. The tunes vary each month, but you'll find familiar tributes like Charles Mingus and John Coltrane on the list. For the closest thing to a jazz club experience (minus the cramped and smoky quarters), attend one of the months with a lively mix like December's Holiday Jazz or February's Jazz for Lovers.

420 S. Tryon St., 704-353-9200
bechtler.org

BE MERRY AND MEDIEVAL
AT THE CAROLINA RENAISSANCE FESTIVAL

Come one, come all to ye olde renaissance festival! Rural North Carolina may not be where you'd expect to find jousting tournaments, royal court characters, or talented jugglers, but at this annual fair on weekends in October and November you have the chance to step back in time. Just north of Charlotte, the festival focuses on medieval times, featuring outdoor theater, crafts, and feasts. Spend an afternoon wandering through period cottages and castles—and more than one hundred vendors offering crafts and food. Live music, performances, and tournaments provide entertainment throughout the day, but simply strolling down the tree-lined streets offers the chance to catch a glimpse of the more than five hundred costumed characters playing their roles around the convivial fest.

16445 Poplar Tent Rd., Huntersville, 704-896-5555
royalfaires.com/carolina

KICK-START YOUR WEEKEND
AT THE EPICENTRE

Once warm weather arrives, there's no place more popular on a Thursday night than Alive After Five in Uptown's EpiCentre complex. The happy hour celebration, which takes place on the center's rooftop, features live music, drink specials, and some of the best people-watching in the city, as hundreds of Uptown workers spill out of their offices and into the party. You should plan on this being a party that continues into the night. The complex is home to numerous bars and clubs, ranging from the laid-back Black Finn and Whiskey River to the more urbane (and expensive) Suite and Bubble nightclubs. Restaurants around the complex offer great options. Try the sushi, Mexican, and Italian dishes for fueling up for a late night on the town.

210 E. Trade St.
epicentrenc.com

EpiCentre isn't your only option for fun on a warm Thursday night. Check out these other celebrations around town.

Alive After Five at Piedmont Town Center

This spring and summer series includes local bands, food, and drink specials.

aliveafterfives.com/piedmont-town-center

Met Live at Metropolitan

Every Thursday night starting in the spring you'll find Greenway-side live music and great sunset views at this casual event.

metropolitanclt.com

Alive After Five at Ballantyne Commons

The South Charlotte crowd flocks to this convenient location for libations and live music on Thursday nights.

aliveafterfives.com/ballantyne-commons

WATCH THE LEONARD BEARSTEIN SYMPHONY
IN FOUNDERS HALL

You should go to the Charlotte Symphony's annual holiday concert, and, yes, most of the local performance venues offer festive seasonal shows, but nothing draws quite as much attention—especially from the younger set—as these beloved animatronic costumed bears in the bustling atrium of Uptown's Founders Hall. The forty-five-minute program, which occurs daily, from 10 A.M. to 8 P.M. throughout December and features songs like "Frosty the Snowman" and "We Wish You a Merry Christmas," has become a local family favorite. The concert is free, so grab a cup of hot chocolate at the adjacent Caribou Coffee and soak in the holiday season.

100 N. Tryon St., 704-716-8649
foundershall.com

RING IN THE NEW YEAR
IN CENTER CITY

3...2...1... Charlotte Center City's New Year's Eve celebration has become a local favorite—especially for families. Held in Romare Bearden Park with its stunning skyline backdrop, the event features singers, aerial artists, mimes, jugglers, and various other cultural performers starting in the early afternoon. In the evening hours, food trucks pull up to offer dinner, as families watch entertainers on the stage. Starting around 10 P.M., the grown-up party gets grooving with a headliner on the main stage and groups gathering to count down to midnight and welcome in the new year. Have someone in tow whose bedtime comes before midnight? No problem. There's a kids' countdown early in the day, so the smallest members of your family can kick off the new year in festive fashion as well.

300 S. Church St., 704-432-4280
charlottecentercity.org

TAKE IN THE TUNES
AT UPTOWN AMPHITHEATRE

When it comes to warm summertime concerts, there's no better spot in town than the Time Warner Cable Uptown Amphitheatre at the NC Music Factory. The venue, which has a capacity of five thousand, offers skyline views from its reserved and lawn seats. This spot consistently draws popular performers—Bob Dylan, OneRepublic, Kesha, and My Morning Jacket have all made stops here in the past. Start your night with local craft beers and oversized soft pretzels in the laid-back beer garden at the adjacent VGBG. Then, after the show, the NC Music Factory offers a variety of bars, restaurants, and nightclubs to end your evening in equally entertaining style.

1000 NC Music Factory Blvd., 704-987-0612
ncmusicfactory.com

ENJOY A FLICK AND FARE
AT STUDIO MOVIE GRILL

Date night just got easier. Forget having to plan several stops for dinner and a movie. EpiCentre's Studio Movie Grill is a restaurant-meets-movie-theater complete with oversized seats, a chef-driven menu, and the chance to order tableside while you watch the latest blockbusters on the big screen. With a menu that includes ceviche lettuce wraps, crab cake sliders with lemon dill aioli, and smoked pork ribs, you don't have to worry about sacrificing flavor for your film viewing. Be sure to keep an eye out for special series, including Family Rewind, featuring classic films from the '80s and '90s, or Girls Night Out, with memorable movies like *Dirty Dancing* and *Footloose* back on the big screen.

210 E. Trade St., 704-972-1062
studiomoviegrill.com

HIT THE CLUBS
FOR CIAA

Some people will tell you that Charlotte's annual CIAA tournament is about basketball. Don't listen to them. This weeklong fan fest may be the city's most event- and celebrity-packed of the year, which makes it the perfect time to see and be seen at Uptown's hottest nightlife destinations. Thousands of visitors flock to the city for the festivities, from fashion shows to concerts—and, of course, the occasional basketball game. Hip hop stars often host parties at clubs in complexes like the NC Music Factory and EpiCentre, while upscale evenings at such spots as the Ritz-Carlton or Harvey B. Gantt Center include politicians, performers, and pro sports stars. For the most up-to-date info on navigating the busy week, keep an eye on *Charlotte Magazine*'s online guide. The publication covers the big events and famous faces around town for the week.

theciaa.com/bballtournament
charlottemagazine.com/ciaa

TIP

For those south of the city,
Cinebarre at the Arboretum offers
the chance to order bites and drinks
from your seat while you
settle in to watch the show.
8008 Providence Rd., 704-543-4582
cinebarre.com

CROON CAROLINA STYLE
AT AN AVETT BROTHERS SHOW

The tunes of famed folk-rock band the Avett Brothers might be Charlotte's most famous export in recent years. The group, composed of brothers Scott and Seth Avett, bassist Bob Crawford, and cellist Joe Kwon, is originally from just outside Charlotte. While the band's songs have received international acclaim and they're frequently on tour around the country, you'll want to catch them when they return to their home state for one of their high-energy shows. They frequently play New Year's Eve shows in the area, often with the Avett brothers' sister, Bonnie, and father, Jim, joining them on stage for some of their more nostalgic songs. While you may have been able to find them in the area's cozier venues a decade ago, these days the band easily fills the city's largest arena with local fans.

theavettbrothers.com

LOOK UP
AT THE AIRPORT OVERLOOK

Pack a snack and head to the overlook at Charlotte Douglas International Airport. The road in is curvy—and very dark at night—and the parking lot is gravel, but the view is more than worth it. In addition to close-up glimpses of the gigantic jets taking off and landing, on a clear night you have gorgeous views of Uptown's skyline lights. Prefer a daytime trip? A grassy area with picnic tables and benches makes for the perfect picnic spot on a sunny afternoon. One of this spot's best attributes might actually be its lack of popularity. Most days this is a quiet spot with only a few other visitors enjoying the view.

7300 Old Dowd Rd.

LINGER LONGER
AT THE COMMON MARKET

The Common Market in Charlotte has two locations, and locals from both neighborhoods would argue over which quirky grocer/ deli/bar/coffee shop/entertainment venue is best. Regardless of whether you prefer South End's airy patio lined in beer signs or the original Plaza Midwood location's cozy bar area with its fifteen craft brews on tap, you'll want to spend some time hanging out in this funky, hip shop. From wine tastings to drag shows, there's always something happening at the Common Market. Stop in for a cup of coffee and neighborhood chat in the morning, or order up one of the tasty sandwiches for a midday lunch. Whenever you go, plan on sticking around for a while. This is the kind of place where you'll want to hang out and soak in the local vibe.

2007 Commonwealth Ave., 704-334-6209
1515 S. Tryon St., 704-332-7782
commonmarketisgood.com

PACK A PICNIC
TO SEE THE SYMPHONY

For summer Sunday evenings in SouthPark, you'll want to stock up on your favorite al fresco dining fare for the Charlotte Symphony's annual Pops in the Park series. Stop in at one of the nearby markets—Whole Foods, Dean and Deluca, and Reid's Fine Foods are all within two miles of the park—and fill a basket with local cheese and charcuterie. Or, for the ultimate spread, such restaurants as the nearby Rooster's Wood-Fired Kitchen or Block & Grinder will prepare a picnic (complete with a bottle of your favorite wine, of course) for you to pick up. Go early to this popular event to snag a patch of grass near the water to enjoy the best acoustics under the stars. If you're only able to make it to one performance, go on July 3 when the orchestra's tunes take on a moving patriotic note in honor of Independence Day.

Symphony Park at SouthPark, 4400 Sharon Rd., 704-972-2000
charlottesymphony.org

CATCH A SHOW
AT THE EVENING MUSE

While this NoDa neighborhood club has only been open since 2001, it's packed a lot of local music history—and great shows—into its time. The one-room venue with a coffee house vibe has featured thousands of acts, ranging from local acoustic guitar soloists to nationally touring stars making a Charlotte stop. With a stage that's seen the likes of the Avett Brothers and Sugarland in their pre–international fame days, it's no wonder a line often stretches down the street to get into the 120-person-capacity spot. Experiencing the Muse for yourself shouldn't be hard. With around seventy artists performing each month, almost every night offers the chance to stop by the cozy corner music destination for a local beer and catch an up-and-coming star.

3227 N. Davidson St., 704-376-3737
eveningmuse.com

RECREATION AND SPORT

PRACTICE YOUR DOWNWARD DOG
WITH A VIEW

Take it outside—your yoga mat and zen attitude, that is. NC Yoga Bar offers outside-the-box, experienced-based yoga events around Charlotte, and the chance to get fit and flexible in an unexpected setting. You can join in weekly classes at spots like Advent Coworking in Plaza Midwood, or keep an eye out for pop up classes in picturesque places like Freedom Park. And Charlotte loves mixing its bends and brews. NC Yoga Bar offers classes at breweries like Sycamore Brewing and Lenny Boy Brewing Co. and you'll also find other seasonal yoga sessions at spots like Olde Mecklenburg Brewery and Unknown Brewery. These may not feature the same views as places like the park, but they do offer the chance to toast your completed workout with a local craft beer.

Ncyogabar.com

FEEL THE SPEED
AT NASCAR HALL OF FAME

Uptown's 150,000-square-foot shrine to the glory of NASCAR offers plenty of thrills for those who are fans of the adrenaline-driven sport. Sit on the edge of your seat in the High Octane Theater, where a sixty-four-foot-wide projection screen and surround sound tell the stories of the often fiery sport, or take a stroll down Glory Road showcasing eighteen famed cars from NASCAR's history. For the ultimate race-day experience, though, buckle up in the iRacing NASCAR stock car simulators. Featuring exact track replicas, these simulators have been tested by such top drivers as Jeff Gordon and Dale Earnhardt Jr. Now it's your turn to hit the road—no helmet or fire suit required.

400 E. Martin Luther King Jr. Blvd., 704-654-4400
nascarhall.com

GET LOST IN THE AMAZING MAIZE MAZE
AT RURAL HILL

As the leaves begin to turn, there's no spot more fun to celebrate autumn than in the gorgeous, rolling pastures of the historic Rural Hill farm. The farm, located just north of town, plays host to many large events throughout the year, but its seven-acre corn maze on weekends in September and October is its most playful—and popular. With more than two miles of connecting paths, including twelve mailboxes containing map pieces, the family-friendly maze is one of the largest in the Southeast. If you're seeking a serious adventure, join in for one of the Friday night after-dark mazes. You'll need a flashlight—and courage—for this trek, but each twist and turn gets you closer to the finish, which is when you can enjoy hayrides, bonfires, food, music, and, of course, your victory.

4431 Neck Rd., Huntersville, 704-875-3113
ruralhill.net

TAKE A RIDE
ON THE BOOTY LOOP

Each year the 24 Hours of Booty charity event ropes off the picturesque roads of this upscale Myers Park neighborhood for cyclists to raise money for cancer research. The riders take the 2.8-mile trip up and down the hood's hills, past Queens University, along the tree-lined Queens Road, and by some of the city's most beautiful homes. The ride lasts for twenty-four hours, but the other 364 days of the year, locals love this circle for walking, jogging, or honing their own criterium skills. Since it's well known, cars in the area are used to seeing cyclists, and the occasional water fountain makes the sidewalks both person and dog friendly. While you'll find runners on this route year-round, the best time to hit these streets is in autumn when Queens Road's large trees turn vivid hues of orange and yellow, making the loop even more striking than usual.

Parking is available at Myers Park Methodist Church (except on Sunday morning), 1501 Queens Rd.

TAKE TO THE TRAILS
FOR A HISTORIC SUNSET HORSEBACK RIDE

Time to channel your inner cowboy. At the picturesque and pastoral Latta Plantation just north of Charlotte, you'll find 1,351 acres of nature preserve on Mountain Island Lake. The historic farm offers hiking, canoeing, kayaking, and picnicking, but the top draw at this circa-1800 cotton plantation may be its equestrian center. From hayrides in the fall to summer camps for kids, the center is a favorite destination for horse lovers. Every other Saturday throughout the year, Latta offers $65 sunset rides, which start with an hour ride around the property and watching the sun set over a pasture, and end with a tasty steak or chicken dinner at the barnside bonfire.

6201 Sample Rd., 704-992-1550
lattaequestriancenter.com

TAKE YOU OUT
TO THE (KNIGHTS) BALL GAME

Get ready for hot dogs and home runs for the home team at a Charlotte Knights game in the team's sleek, new Uptown stadium. BB&T Ballpark, which opened in 2014, has ten thousand seats—and there's not a bad one in the house. Every seat offers stunning skyline views and, oh, also a pretty decent view of the evening's minor league game or entertainment. Plus, whether you're dropping in for lunch and a few innings or settling in for the evening, the park's food and drink offerings are something to cheer about as well. Forget the peanuts and order up a pulled pork potato from Queen City Q, featuring a baked potato stuffed with barbecue, queso, and green onions—and only available at the park. For the full Southern summer experience, wash it all down with one of the cold local craft beers served in a mason jar.

324 S. Mint St., 704-357-8071
milb.com

SPEND THE NIGHT
IN A TREE HOUSE

Don't worry, these are a far cry from the rustic tree houses of your youth. At the locally owned and run Treehouse Vineyards in Monroe, you can sip the wine made from grapes grown on-site while enjoying the evening in a private—and luxurious—tree house. One tree house, which is thirty feet off the ground, features an outdoor fireplace and two porches, available for hourly rental and perfect for soaking in the countryside with a chilled glass of vino in hand. The other house, which overlooks the pond and vineyards, is offered for overnight stays and includes a kitchenette, full bath, and bedroom. Plus, the winery's tasting room features muscadine juices, ciders, and even slushies, all perfect accompaniments for your adventurous evening outdoors.

301 Bay St., 704-283-4208
treehousevineyards.net

MAKE A SPLASH
IN DANIEL STOWE BOTANICAL GARDENS

Just west of Charlotte is 380 acres of thick forests, grassy pastures, and manicured gardens. Open year-round, this gorgeous destination is worth a visit anytime. Even in the middle of winter, you'll find a warm, wet conservatory filled with tropical orchid blooms and colorful plants. The best time to visit, though, is in the spring when the entire garden is awash with color. Stroll down brick paths filled with fragrant flowers, and rest in the shade of wooden arbors and trellises covered in Southern vines. The garden is ideal for picnics with the family, and children especially love its playful fountains, where they can splash in the cool water on warm days. Also be sure to stop by the garden's gift shop on your way out. Filled with books on gardening, botanical-inspired jewelry, and locally made goods, like jams and candles, it's the perfect spot for a souvenir from your day meandering the garden paths.

6500 S. New Hope Rd., Belmont, 704-825-4490
dsbg.org

TAKE A TWIRL
ON UPTOWN'S ICE RINK

The coolest spot in town each December is Holiday on Ice on the NASCAR Hall of Fame Plaza. Pack your extra hats and hand warmers because whether you're a Wayne Gretzky wannabe, an amateur, or just a kid, this is the frozen hot spot for the holiday season. With more than seven thousand square feet of ice, the outdoor rink decked in twinkling white lights offers scenic Uptown skyline views while you figure-eight your way around the ice. Open Thanksgiving through New Year's, the rink features special events, including Wednesday Date Night with couples skates and evening appearances by Santa Claus. Admission is $9, and admission with skate rental is $12. Your best investment here, though, may be a rinkside cup of hot cocoa to indulge in after your loops around the ice.

400 E. Martin Luther King Jr. Blvd.
holidayonice.com

KAYAK TO CRAFT BEER
ON THE CATAWBA

Grab a paddle and your sense of adventure because this isn't your typical evening of dining. On the U.S. National Whitewater Center's Microbrews Cruises, which are offered May through October, you'll have to work for your dinner. First, you'll hop on a kayak and paddle up the Catawba River, where a guide will lead your group along the smooth, blue water and into a wooded creek area as the sun is sinking. After approximately an hour of kayaking, the group returns to the center, where dinner has been prepared around a large campfire on wooded Hawk Island. Now comes the really fun part. Each week a different craft brewery serves up its beer pairings to accompany the dinner, so you'll have the chance to sample seasonal brews as a brewery representative shares the story and flavors behind the beer.

5000 Whitewater Center Pkwy., 704-391-3900
usnwc.org

TIP

Bring a change of clothes on your microbrew cruise. What you wear to kayak will get wet, and once the sun sets, you'll want to be wearing something warm to gather around the fire and linger over your dinner and brews.

SLIP AND SLIDE
AT GREAT WOLF LODGE

Get ready to get wet! This playful resort just outside of town is focused on adventure, and in no place is that more obvious than in its eighty-thousand-square-foot water park, featuring slides, geysers, and even suspension bridges. Set at eighty-four degrees, this year-round park includes three swimming pools and a four-story tree house with a one-thousand-gallon bucket at the top tipping out water throughout the day. This spot is as family friendly as they come. Certain pools and slides are reserved for younger kids, while the indoor facility even includes a gaming center for teenagers not in the mood to swim.

10175 Weddington Rd., Concord, 704-549-8206
greatwolf.com

CHEER ON MARATHONERS
AT THUNDER ROAD RACE

Whether you're a hardcore runner or just someone who enjoys a good mimosa in the morning, this annual race is one you'll want to watch (or run). If you're not hitting the pavement for 26.2 miles, find a spot alongside the route to cheer on local runners for the city's marathon. The run, which begins in Uptown, takes runners through the Myers Park, SouthPark, Dilworth, NoDa, and Plaza Midwood neighborhoods, so there's no shortage of spots for settling in streetside. Groups holding posters, toasting runners, and playing music cheer along the entire route. To catch more runners, find a spot in one of the neighborhoods south of town, where the half marathoners make their way as well. To see the seriously impressive athletes, though, set up camp in NoDa or Plaza Midwood, which are the last of the miles for the marathoners.

runcharlotte.com

REV YOUR ENGINES
AT THE RICHARD PETTY DRIVING EXPERIENCE

Have a need for speed? Buckle up for the Richard Petty Driving Experience. You have the option to be the one with your foot on the gas or sit back in the front seat for a ride-along in the heart of NASCAR land. While driving in a six-hundred-horsepower NASCAR race car with four-speed manual transmission will get your heart racing, the ride-along allows for its own rush. For $59, you'll travel shotgun with a pro for three laps at top speeds of 165 miles per hour around the 1.5-mile quad-oval track at the Charlotte Motor Speedway. Can't resist the driver's seat? For prices starting at $449, you can take an eight- to fifty-lap spin on your own around the course.

5555 Concord Pkwy., Concord, 800-237-3889
drivepetty.com

HIT THE LINKS
AT THE WELLS FARGO CHAMPIONSHIP

Since its debut in 2003, this PGA Tour stop has drawn some of golf's top names with such winners as Tiger Woods, Rory McIlroy, and Rickie Fowler. While the tournament itself is impressive—the course is known to have one of the hardest finishes with holes 16, 17, and 18 being known as the Green Mile—there's plenty more than golf to entertain at this tournament. Sprawling mansions dot the course of the Quail Hollow Country Club, and attendees and golfers mingle in its elegant clubhouse and well-manicured grounds throughout the weekend. If you're looking for the best view of the golf, head to the second floor of the Champions Club, which overlooks the eighth green. From this breezy perch, you can catch close-ups of your favorite players while enjoying a cold drink in the shade.

3700 Gleneagles Rd., 704-554-8161
wellsfargochampionship.com

TIP

After a day of traipsing around the
course, head to Del Frisco's Steakhouse
in SouthPark, where the bar, patio,
and dining room are always packed
with fellow fans catching up
on the day's hits and misses.
4725 Piedmount Row Dr. #170
704-552-5502
delfriscos.com/charlotte

SWIM WITH OLYMPIANS
AT THE AQUATIC CENTER

Ryan Lochte trains there. Cullen Jones trains there. Michael Phelps swims there. Charlotte's uptown aquatic center is a hot spot for the country's coolest swimmers to show off their strokes. The natatorium includes a 50-meter competitive pool, 25-yard therapeutic pool, fitness center, and a hot tub. And in 2015 it closed for around a year to undergo an $8.6 million renovation to become a state-of-the-art spot to take a dip. But luckily, no medals are required for making a splash. Daily rates and memberships are available for jumping in anytime.

800 E Martin Luther King Jr Blvd., 704-336-3483
charmeck.org

BITE INTO A FOOTLONG AND FRIED PICKLES
AT THE DIAMOND

No venture into Charlotte's culinary scene is complete without a trip to this Plaza Midwood landmark. The legendary diner, which has been serving up Southern comfort food to locals since 1945, features a red neon sign, food served in paper baskets, and a laid-back ambience. Its storied history, which includes twin brother owners in the 1960s and Greek immigrant Gerry Pistiolis in the 1980s, is reflected in its varied menu. Diners with hearty appetites can dig into decadent dishes like gravy fries, deep fried chicken livers, and hot pimento cheese dip. But for the ultimate iconic experience, order the footlong Diamond Dog loaded with chili, mustard, and onions alongside the famed fried pickles and wash it down with a tall, cold can of PBR beer. You'll understand why the line is out the door most nights at this laid-back neighborhood spot.

1901 Commonwealth Ave., 704-375-8959
diamond charlotte.com

CATCH A MATCH
AT COURTYARD HOOLIGANS

At bars all over town, you can watch NFL, NBA, or MLB on the big screens, but when it comes to catching the latest soccer match, there's no place with as many matches—or as much European-style charm—as this cozy bar. Nestled between skyscrapers and tucked into Uptown's historic Brevard Court behind Latta Arcade, Courtyard Hooligans is the ideal soccer pub. Team flags adorn the walls, and the laid-back bar offers both local craft brews and European favorites to enjoy while you cheer on your team. Whether you're a die-hard fan of the English Premier League or just enjoy watching the occasional Major League Soccer match, you're likely to find fellow fans here. Since most of the games are played overseas, the bar frequently fills up in the afternoon or even mornings with serious sports fans hoping to see their team live.

140 Brevard Ct., 704-376-2238
facebook.com/courtyardhooligans

PREGAME
FOR THE PANTHERS
IN THEIR LAIR

These days, with their recent winning record and newly renovated stadium, it's not hard to get pumped up for a Carolina Panthers game. The local NFL team is a fan favorite in Charlotte, and on game days all eyes in the city are on Bank of America Stadium to cheer for the home team. Chances are, if you're going to the game, you've been tailgating long before kickoff. To really get into the spirit, though, head to the Panthers Lair near the south and east gates of the stadium, where free pregame festivities rev up fans two hours before game time. The TopCat cheerleaders and Sir Purr mascot make appearances—and offer autographs and photos. Plus, you can have your face painted, win prizes, and start cheering early for the team at this family-friendly event.

800 S. Mint St., 704-358-7000
panthers.com

BACK THE BUZZ
AT A HORNETS GAME

When Charlotte got its first NBA team in 1988, they were known as the Charlotte Hornets—and they were huge. Fans packed the house in the coliseum just outside of town to see such players as Dell Curry and Muggsy Bogues. In 2002 the Hornets moved to New Orleans, and in 2004 the Charlotte Bobcats were established and began playing in Uptown's Time Warner Cable Arena in 2005. They've never had quite the draw, though, until now. The Bobcats have taken back the Hornets name starting in the 2014–2015 season, and local hoops fans can't get enough. Buy a ticket, but don't plan on sitting much in that seat. In this buzzing coliseum, you'll be on your feet cheering all night.

333 E. Trade St.
nba.com/hornets

GET SPOOKED
AT SCAROWINDS

For most of the year, Carowinds Amusement Park just south of town offers its thrills in the form of almost four hundred acres of swooping roller coasters, gushing water chutes, and playful children's rides. For weekends in the fall, the park transforms to terrorize anyone who dares to enter. The PG-13 experience includes five Scare Zones, where more than five hundred vampires, monsters, and the like are stationed to frighten passersby. Fear-seekers will also find live shows and rides with Halloween themes, but the most chilling part of an evening here is inside one of the eight mazes, which each have their own gruesome theme, ranging from a haunted insane asylum to a top-secret military facility. Happy haunting!

14523 Carowinds Blvd., 704-588-2600
carowinds.com

TIP

Carowinds is serious about that PG-13 rating. While some areas are more kid friendly and plenty of squealing teenagers have fun, this event is definitely geared toward adults.

CATCH THE *CATAWBA QUEEN* ON LAKE NORMAN

Who needs the Mississippi? At Queens Landing on Lake Norman, those who want to set sail can hop aboard the *Catawba Queen*, a replica of a riverboat. The two-story boat, which features a full bar, is available for lunch and dinner cruises around the man-made lake. In addition to discussing the lake's history, the captain shares the juicy details on who lives in the sprawling lakeside mansions (spoiler: it's mostly NASCAR drivers). While the casual ninety-minute lunch ride is a great way to see the lake, the sunset cruise is your best bet for picturesque views—and photos—of one of the region's most scenic spots.

1459 River Hwy., 704-663-2628
queenslanding.com

PUT ON YOUR PASTELS
FOR THE QUEEN'S CUP STEEPLECHASE

In the spring, there's no place to see and be seen quite like the Queen's Cup. This annual horse race set on rolling green farmland just south of Charlotte features brightly dressed jockeys, magnificent thoroughbred horses, and spectators decked out in their Southern best. Women wearing sundresses and dramatic hats mingle under tents over cocktails and picnic fare with men in bowties and khakis. Most of the tailgating fun happens in the moderately priced infield parking, but this is one event worth the splurge. For the ultimate race—and style—experience, choose Member's Hill and Paddock, where your tickets include chef-prepared multicourse meals, an open bar, and live music.

6103 Waxhaw Hwy., Mineral Springs
queenscup.org

CRUISE THROUGH CENTER CITY
VIA SEGWAY

Ready to cover some serious Charlotte ground? Strap on your helmet, lean forward, and hit the streets on a Segway. Charlotte NC Tours offers a variety of versions of Segwaying options, including an after-dark Haunted Tour through Settlers Cemetery; a Taste & Glide Tour, with stops at popular Uptown and South End restaurants; and a Markets, Museums & Parks Tour. Your best bet, though, for the quick and dirty on Center City is the one-hour fun ride. The ride, which takes you down Uptown's wide sidewalks, makes stops at the city's top museums, the Green, historic Fourth Ward, and the bustling intersection of Trade and Tryon Streets, is just $40.

704-962-4548
charlottenctours.com/segwaytours

TAKE FLIGHT
IN A CHARLOTTE HELICOPTER TOUR

Go above and beyond for a unique look at the city with local tours offered by Thrillant Adventure Sports. These luxe rides, which take off from the neighboring towns of Waxhaw or Gastonia, fly over Charlotte's Uptown and hover near the area's more interesting views (think Bank of America Stadium or the NASCAR Hall of Fame). Whether you want to enjoy a romantic sunset voyage or an after-dark skyline view is up to you. For $799 for one hour, two riders can pick their own time to take in the city—and enjoy a complimentary champagne toast to the town as they fly.

thrillant.com

SCALE AN UPTOWN
SKYSCRAPER

Attention, adrenaline junkies: each fall Special Olympics North Carolina offers the chance to rappel down more than twenty stories of an Uptown skyscraper. The event, which has been held at the Vue condominiums and Fifth Third Center in the past, costs $1,000 to enter, with all the funds raised going to the charity. Thrill-seekers generally raise funds for the daring drop in a full-body harness. You'll get a quick instruction session (and, of course, plenty of safety equipment) before you drop from the top. It takes about fifteen minutes, which actually feels like a remarkably long time when you're dangling hundreds of feet in the air.

sonc.net

PADDLE AROUND
ON LAKE NORMAN

Get ready to get wet! During warm months, My Aloha Paddle and Surf offers private and group stand-up paddleboard lessons for beginners on the lake. You'll have the chance to learn how to balance, turn, and glide on the boards, all while working on your core—and your tan. And if you like it—or if you're already not a novice—the shop and school also offers challenging fitness classes combining paddleboarding with yoga and pilates poses. Plus, the shop has locations in Mooresville and Cornelius, where you can rent both the boards and kayaks, which means you're all out of excuses for not getting fit while you have fun on the water.

584 Brawley School Rd., 704-526-8432
standuplkn.com

PUSH PEDALS
ON THE GREENWAY

Between B-Cycle bike share and the city's Greenway, urban cycling in Charlotte is as easy as, well, riding a bike. Rent one of the cycles at the Metropolitan station in Midtown and hop on the Little Sugar Creek Greenway. This gorgeous green stretch offers miles of winding waterside bike trails and skyline views with park benches alongside, perfect for stopping for a picnic or just to rest your legs. Ride into Freedom Park, where you can take a stroll around the seven-acre lake before returning your bike to one of the convenient stations after an afternoon of exploring on two wheels.

charlotte.bcycle.com

HIKE PINNACLE TRAIL
ON A CLEAR DAY

When an afternoon is cloud free, hikers in Crowders Mountain State Park can see the Charlotte skyline from one side of King's Pinnacle and the blue peaks of the Appalachian Mountains from the other. The four-mile-round-trip trail, which starts at the park office, is moderately difficult for the first part and turns rocky and into a steeper incline for the last bit. Every step is worth it, however, once you're standing over the sheer cliffs and checking out the spectacular view. You're only half an hour outside Charlotte, but any stress of city life feels far removed from these beautiful woods.

522 Park Office Lane, Kings Mountain, 704-853-5375
ncparks.gov/visit/parks/crmo

ZIPLINE AND DINE
AT THE WHITEWATER CENTER

Hold on tight! At the U.S. National Whitewater Center's Wednesday night Zipline & Dine, for $75 you can zip through the trees as the sun sets before toasting your bravery with fireside dinner and drinks. The lines, which loop between trees alongside the Catawba River, include five zip lines and two roped bridges before you rappel to the ground and hike back to base camp. The seasonal dinners, which are chef prepared, include two drinks of your choice (craft beer or wine). While always a thrilling evening, the best time of year for this combination is in the fall when you'll be gliding through gorgeous, colorful leaves before returning to cozy up next to the roaring fire pit.

5000 Whitewater Center Pkwy., 704-391-3900
usnwc.org

GLIDE OVER LAKE NORMAN
IN A HOT AIR BALLOON

Lake Norman tends to be scenic from any view, but the best one may be from one thousand feet above. Drift along in a gentle breeze over the pristine lake and its surrounding neighborhoods in a brightly colored giant balloon and basket with Balloons Over Charlotte. If you're an early riser, sunrise is ideal for catching glimpses of nature from above. But the best time for this $185-per-person warm weather excursion may be just before the sun sets when the quiet of the floating balloon offers the chance to focus on panoramic sunset views as you rise into the sky.

704-614-2118
balloonsovercharlotte.com

ROLL RETRO STYLE
AT TEN PARK LANES

Lace up your bowling shoes and bring your competitive spirit because at this old-school alley on Montford Drive you'll be knocking down the pins all night. Originally opened in 1960, this historic bowling alley got an upscale upgrade in 2012. Now, in addition to state-of-the-art lanes, visitors will find a full menu featuring Southern comfort food like burgers and barbecue, as well as three full-service bars. For a seriously Southern experience with a creative twist, try one of the Que Stacked Mason Jars featuring pork, slaw, and baked beans all served in a mason jar. Then wash it all down—and toast your scores postgame—by partaking in the spot's signature selection of moonshine.

1700 Montford Dr., 704-523-7633
rollten.com

PICK STRAWBERRIES
AT HALL FAMILY FARM

There's nothing that says springtime in the South like plucking your own warm, red berries in a local strawberry patch. At Hall Family Farm in South Charlotte, you can buy buckets of ripe, lush prepicked berries or head to the one-acre field to reach under the green leaves and grab them yourself right off the vine. After gathering your haul of the sweet, juicy fruit, there's plenty more to pick up on your way out. The farm also sells honey from its next-door beekeeper, cider made with local muscadines, icy slushies, and irresistible hot funnel cakes. Can't make it in the spring? Stop by in the fall for pumpkin picking and hayrides accompanied by hot cocoa or coffee.

10713 Providence Rd., 704-562-4021
hallfamilyfarm.com

FEED THE OSTRICHES AND OTHER ANIMALS
AT LAZY 5 RANCH

Pick a sunny day for this oversized petting zoo. You'll want all the windows down in your car as you drive the 3.5 miles of road holding more than 750 exotic animals on 185 acres. On this safari-like experience just north of Charlotte, you cruise through grassy meadows filled with various animals, including giraffes, rhinoceroses, and camels, and these guys aren't shy. Roll down your window and you're likely to have an ostrich pop his head in searching for food. For an even more hands-on experience, choose the open-air wagon ride around the property. It lasts approximately an hour and a half and offers a perfect opportunity to slow down and watch the ranch's most popular attraction—its majestic giraffes.

15100 Mooresville Rd., 704-663-5100
lazy5ranch.com

CULTURE
AND HISTORY

LINE UP FOR THE LIGHTS
IN MCADENVILLE

Known as Christmas Town USA, McAdenville, just a few miles west of Charlotte, lights up every December. The tiny town, which has fewer than a thousand residents, draws more than half a million visitors each winter to see its twinkling lights. The lights are strung in trees, on homes, and over streets, and after 5:30 P.M. McAdenville sparkles with the largest light display in the United States. Hundreds of wreaths adorn local lampposts, a life-size Nativity draws crowds, and a display of Santa and his reindeer add to the charm. As you drive through, you're likely to hear carols chiming from the local church bells and see the colorful light show on the Christmassy village's fountain. To check out the merry and bright scene, you'll want to set aside some time. Lines start on nearby Interstate 85 to take the car trip through town. So pack your hot cocoa, turn up the holiday tunes, and enjoy the drive.

McAdenville, mcadenville-christmastown.com

CATCH A RIDE
ON THE GOLD RUSH TROLLEY

Want to soak in the sights of Uptown Charlotte? Hop on one of the Gold Rush Trolleys. Designed to look like the city's historic streetcars and named after the city's famed gold rush, the trolley service offers a circulating line through Center City with frequent stops on Trade Street. It's an easy-to-navigate—and completely free—way to get around some of the city's busiest streets and top attractions during the day. While the trolley-like buses featuring wooden benches and wide windows are often full with local workers on weekday mornings and evenings, they're perfect for visitors and locals to catch a ride midday between Uptown museums, restaurants, and shops.

Trade St., Elizabeth Ave., Fourth St., and Beatties Ford Rd.
charmeck.org

SNAG A BEHIND-THE-CURTAIN TICKET
TO OFF BROADWAY AT BLUMENTHAL

As if being an audience member for Broadway's biggest shows like *The Book of Mormon* or *The Lion King* weren't enough, now you can grab a group and get a serious close-up of the New York City exports with a postshow tour at Uptown's Blumenthal Performing Arts Center. The private peek at the touring productions includes a meet-and-greet with the cast and crew (with questions encouraged) plus the chance to experience workshops on topics like makeup and music. Just being backstage at the Blumenthal offers its own draw with its impressive theatrical equipment and soaring space. The tour, which lasts one hour, is just $15 in addition to your ticket cost. With new musicals arriving throughout the year, keep an eye on the website for visiting stars and especially exciting performances.

130 N. Tryon St., 704-379-1000
blumenthalarts.org

DRESS TO THRILL
AT NODAWEEN

Grab your most gruesome garb and hit the artsy streets of the NoDa neighborhood for this annual Halloween celebration, with a portion of the proceeds going to a local charity. The event, which is hosted by the NoDa Neighborhood and Business Association on the Saturday before Halloween, includes kid-friendly festivities, a costumed 5K run, an evening party at a local brewery, and a screening of *The Rocky Horror Picture Show* in the popular Neighborhood Theatre. The entire afternoon and evening is distinctly NoDa, which is known for its quirky galleries, local live music, and craft beers. The Freaky 5K may be the most popular part of the day, as it takes place at dusk with runners donning costumes ranging from the Mario Brothers to giant French fries, and every runner receives a free beer from a local brewery to toast the end of the race—and the start of a night of NoDaWEEN partying.

NoDa Neighborhood, Thirty-sixth and N. Davidson St.
nodaween.com

SKETCH A LIVE MODEL
AT GALLERY TWENTY-TWO

Time to channel your inner Parisian Left Bank artist. At Plaza Midwood's sleek Gallery Twenty-Two, figure drawing classes draw eclectic crowds. The gallery, which includes a wine and craft-beer bar, features rotating diverse exhibits from local artists on its walls—perfect for inspiring creativity. Stop in most nights and you'll find trendy locals lingering in front of edgy art and comparing hard-to-find brews on draft, but on Monday nights the scene gets especially hip when the gallery drapes curtains across its sidewalk windows and a live, nude model poses in the center of the room as artists take to their sketchpads. The class is free so grab a pint, find one of the soft chairs, and take pencil to paper.

1500 Central Ave., 704-334-0122
gallerytwentytwo.com

GET INVIGORATED ABOUT INNOVATION
AT PACKARD PLACE

Charlotte has long had an entrepreneurial spirit (see the skyline filled with banking skyscrapers), but nowhere is that more apparent than at Packard Place. This ninety-thousand-square-foot Uptown building was designed to be a home for start-up businesses and creative organizations and may be the most inventive spot in Charlotte. Lucky for you, it's easy to access all this entrepreneurial activity. Packard Place hosts various events open to the public almost every day. Sign up for the center's email and you'll receive invites for information sessions, pitching opportunities, and networking events. Whether you're a budding businessperson or just curious about creative minds at work in the city, this building is worth a visit.

222 S. Church St.
packardplace.us

CATCH A FLICK
AT THE MINT MUSEUM

The city's largest art museum features collections and works likely to draw you in for hours. With visiting shows from such cities as New York and Washington, D.C., there's never a shortage of new exhibits for fine art fanatics, but one of the best times for a visit to the Mint is for its frequent viewings of films you're unlikely to find anywhere else. The screenings, which are located at the Mint's Randolph Road location and are $5, are designed to encourage thought and discussion. Make sure to set aside a few minutes before the show to explore the location itself. An original branch of the United States Mint, this museum opened in 1936 as North Carolina's first art museum.

2730 Randolph Rd. and 500 S. Tyron St., 704-337-2000
mintmuseum.org

TIP

If you want to visit the Mint's extensive galleries, do it at a discount. While admission to either location is typically $10 per visit, plan your trip for a Wednesday when it is free from 5 to 9 P.M.

GO BEHIND THE MASK
AT THE HARVEY B. GANTT CENTER

Uptown's Harvey B. Gantt Center for African-American Arts + Culture features a variety of colorful and gorgeous works of art—and will likely inspire you to want to create your own. No problem. In a single session, Portraits, Images & Masks, workshop students have the opportunity to mimic the ceremonial masks created around the world. Your final tangible product from the $450 class is a three-dimensional textured mask, but you'll gain a much deeper understanding of the sociology and communities behind these traditional works of art. Of course, if hands-on isn't your thing, there are plenty of galleries and exhibits to see in this bright and modern building—and a gift shop brimming with finds means you'll still have something to take home from the experience.

551 S. Tryon St., 704-374-1565
ganttcenter.org

STOP AND SMELL THE ROSES
IN MCGILL ROSE GARDEN

For lovers of lush landscapes and verdant respites from urban life, Charlotte offers several gorgeous gardens, but none come with quite the story or bevy of blossoms that you'll find at McGill Rose Garden just outside of Uptown. The small public garden, which was once a coal yard, is almost entirely roses. Guests can stroll down one of the fragrant paths or pause at a park bench to soak in the sight of more than a thousand bushes (and more than two hundred varieties). Be sure to let your wandering lead you to the corner of the garden where, in a testament to its past, a coal car rests in the shade on a piece of railroad track.

940 N. Davidson St., 704-333-6497
mcgillrosegarden.com

DISCOVER A DIFFERENT ERA
AT THE DUNHILL

Pack your bags! There's no better spot for a swank staycation than Uptown's Southern boutique hotel. The ten-story Dunhill, which first opened in 1929 as the Mayfair Manor apartments, features a neoclassical facade and eighteenth-century furnishings, including four-poster beds, elegant draperies, and marble floors. Splurge on the lavish penthouse suite, which includes a luxe fireplace and old-fashioned stone balconies with alluring views of North Tryon Street. Plan on dining at the hotel's chic street-front restaurant, the Asbury, which serves sophisticated and locally sourced dishes for breakfast, lunch, and dinner. And end your evening at the lobby's classic bar with one of its potent martinis perfect for toasting in any era.

237 N. Tryon St., 704-332-4141
dunhillhotel.com

TAKE A WALK WITH LEVINE MUSEUM
OF THE NEW SOUTH

A trip to this Uptown history museum offers an interactive peek into post–Civil War Southern history. At its permanent exhibit, "Cotton Fields to Skyscrapers: Charlotte and the Carolina Piedmont in the New South," you'll find creative displays. See a civil rights–era lunch counter and a one-room tenant farmer's house. To get really up close and personal with Charlotte's rich history, however, become a member and plan your visit around one of the spring walking tours, which include streetcar-era neighborhoods like Dilworth, as well as Uptown spots like Romare Bearden Park. Or, visit in December for the History + Holiday Lights tour which takes a ride through historic neighborhoods to view the festive decor as you hear the local stories.

200 E. Seventh St., 704-333-1887
museumofthenewsouth.org

GO TO THE BIRDS
AT THE CAROLINA RAPTOR CENTER

Don't call it a zoo. This is a fifty-seven-acre rehabilitation center for more than twenty-five species of orphaned and injured raptors, which means that these majestic eagles, owls, falcons, hawks, and more are only in captivity because for some reason they're unable to survive in the wild on their own. Guests can take a short, self-guided walk down a nature trail to view the resident birds, which all have fascinating stories detailing how they arrived at this center just north of town. Ultimately, though, it's just viewing these noble birds of prey up close that's the real thrill for visitors of any age. Stop by on the weekend for bird presentations and flight shows as well as tours of the Eagle Research Observatory.

6000 Sample Rd., Huntersville, 704-875-6521
carolinaraptorcenter.org

CATCH A CARRIAGE
AROUND UPTOWN

OK, so we're not exactly a quaint village of cobblestone streets, but there's still something charming about taking a private horse-drawn Victorian carriage down the skyscraper-lined streets of Uptown. Grab a hot cup of coffee at 7th Street Public Market or The King's Bakery, and then line up for a cool evening in the city. Southern Breezes Carriages starts its twenty-minute weekend carriage tours on Tryon Street between Sixth and Seventh Streets. From there, the white-wheeled tours clip-clop through the Fourth Ward neighborhood, past historic homes and parks, and then take a spin around Uptown. Feeling spontaneous? No reservations are needed for these tours, which are on a first-come, first-served basis.

704-301-5111
southernbreezes.com

GET IN ON THE FOOD AND FUN
AT THE GREEK FESTIVAL

There's a Greek word for when the music is playing and you're consumed with the joys of life: *kefi*. Charlotte's annual Yiasou Greek Festival in September is brimming with *kefi*. Launched in the 1970s, the festival attracts more than five thousand people each year to Dilworth's Holy Trinity Greek Orthodox Church for cultural lectures, music, dancing, art, shopping, and, of course, Greek fare. The gyros and spanakopitas are favorites, but don't leave without trying the honey-drenched baklava. If you're short on time but looking for a Greek food fix, the festival even offers a drive-through to pick up the tasty dinners, sandwiches, and desserts.

600 East Blvd.
yiasoufestival.org

EXPLORE
OVERSTREET MALL'S TUNNELS

Urban planners could argue for hours on the pros and cons of Uptown's system of bridges, sidewalks, and hidden shops that compose the Overstreet Mall system. Regardless of your sentiments on city design, this unusual series of interior walkways connects coffee shops, boutiques, performance centers, restaurants, bars, office space, hotels, parking, and even residences, which makes it unlike anything else you'll find in town—or in the Southeast for that matter. Many entrances are handy, and Hearst Tower or EpiCentre are good spots to start, but serious city navigators will tell you that there are routes entirely by interior walkways that start as far south on Tryon as the Duke Energy Town. While you could likely spend an entire day meandering through shops and stopping in restaurants, you'll find that the mall is busiest at lunchtime when Uptown workers hurry through its halls to grab a bite between meetings.

charlotteoverstreetmall.com

POLISH UP YOUR ACTING SKILLS
AT A LOCAL SHOOT

Charlotte may not be the East Coast answer to Hollywood yet, but we're getting our fair share of filming these days. Most notably in recent years you could find Claire Danes and Mandy Patinkin around town shooting scenes for the hit Showtime series *Homeland*. Before that the big news was having the first of the *Hunger Games* trilogy filmed in our fair city. These days locals barely blink an eye at network pilots and movies being made. Want to get in on the action? Sign up to be an extra with Tona B. Dahlquist Casting. This local agency casts extras for the city's biggest productions and frequently has last-minute openings for upcoming scenes—no experience needed. If you're ready to hang with the stars for a day, follow the agency on Facebook and Twitter to see what they're seeking for the latest shoot.

facebook.com/Tona-B-Dahlquist-Casting, @2CastU

WITNESS THE MIRACLE
ON THE HUDSON

When US Airways Flight 1549 struck a flock of geese and was forced to land in New York's Hudson River, it was on its way to Charlotte. So it's only appropriate that the plane's final resting place is at the Carolinas Aviation Museum near the Charlotte airport. The exhibit, which was opened with a speech from the famous Captain Chesley B. "Sully" Sullenberger and invitations to the 155 passengers, features the damaged airframe, fuselage, wings, and engines. Videos, photos, and items from the aircraft round out this fascinating exhibit, which tells the story of what has been called history's most successful ditching of an airliner.

4672 First Flight Dr., 704-359-8442
carolinasaviation.org

EXPLORE THE RAIN FOREST
AT DISCOVERY PLACE

There's no shortage of ways to have a little nerdy fun at Charlotte's science museum. From technology learning labs to aquariums, the Uptown museum features state-of-the-art offerings for anyone with a penchant for innovation. One of the hottest parts of the museum, though, is its iconic tropical rain forest. The atrium, which features waterfalls and plants, is kept at a balmy eighty-five degrees and has more than twenty-five different species of animals—all individually named. Kids (of all ages) get the chance to learn about the ecosystem and even pet a few of the animals. For even more fun, plan your visit for one of the museum's Friday night "Science on the Rocks" events. The evenings, which are open to ages 21 and up, feature the chance to view the museums's latest exhibits—with a drink in hand.

301 N. Tryon St., 704-372-6261
discoveryplace.org

STROLL DOWN MAIN STREET
IN DAVIDSON

Looking for some small-town charm? Just north of the city, Davidson is part college town, part historic haven. Start your day here with a steaming mug of coffee on one of the sidewalk benches at Summit Coffee. From there, explore the galleries, boutiques, and restaurants that line the quaint Main Street. Be sure to stop in Main Street Books, where shelves are stacked with local literature. The street also runs by the well-manicured campus of Davidson College, where you can wander between tall brick buildings dedicated to higher learning. By far the best time to visit, though, is on a summer Saturday when the Davidson Farmers Market fills up South Main Street with local vendors selling their wares, chef demonstrations, and families mingling over the fresh food.

Summit Coffee, 128 S. Main St., Davidson
704-895-9090, summitcoffee.com
Main Street Books, 126 S. Main St., Davidson
704-892-6841, facebook.com/main-street-books-davidson
Davidson College, 405 N. Main St., Davidson
704-894-2000, davidson.edu
Davidson Farmers Market, 120 S. Main St., Davidson
704-400-0880, davidsonfarmersmarket.org

**Feel like checking out
other area farmers markets?
Here are prime places for picking up
locally grown, raised, and made fare.**

Charlotte Regional Farmers Market

Open year-round and operated by the North Carolina
Department of Agriculture, this is the granddaddy of
local markets. Keep an eye out for the Local Farm,
Local Food flags to make sure you're getting the
regional produce, cheese, and veggies.

180 Yorkmont Rd.
704-357-1269
ncagr.gov/markets/facilities/markets/charlotte

Kings Drive Farmers Market

This centrally located market fills up fast on Saturday mornings in the spring, summer, and fall with locals looking for fresh vegetables, eggs, meats, and flowers. It's also a prime spot for pumpkins in October and Christmas trees in December.

938 S. Kings Dr.
704-332-6366
facebook.com/simpsons-produce

Common Grounds Farm Stand

Yes, it's small, but this community farm stand in Myers Park offers local, organic, and homemade items, and benefits the local charity, Urban Ministry Center. So you get to shop for fresh fare in a charming spot, and your money goes to helping the homeless. Win-win.

119 Huntley Pl.
704-334-1613
commongroundsfarmstand.org

WALK THROUGH HISTORY
AT THE BILLY GRAHAM LIBRARY

Famed evangelist Billy Graham was born and raised in Charlotte, where he later built the Billy Graham Evangelistic Association. While Graham is one of the world's most well-known Christian ministers and his eponymous public library is focused on promoting his faith, it's also designed for history buffs of any religion. Built to look like a dairy barn reminiscent of the one where Graham grew up, the library features a self-guided tour, including multimedia presentations portraying his fascinating life as well as Graham's authentically restored childhood home. Plan your visit for a pleasant day, and stop by the peaceful and flower-filled Memorial Prayer Garden near the gravesite of Graham's wife, Ruth Bell Graham.

4330 Westmont Dr., 704-401-3200
billygrahamlibrary.org

SOLVE A MURDER MYSTERY
AT THEATRE CHARLOTTE

This volunteer-based community theater tucked in the Myers Park neighborhood is one of the most vibrant companies in the city, staging impressive—and often timely—productions each season. While its main shows do draw crowds, its Murder Mystery Series is your best bet for experiencing the creative cast of characters behind this venue. The evenings, which are accompanied by catered dinners, have you teamed with your table to figure out whodunit from the cast of suspects by the end of the night. Just don't forget to take a break from the investigation to bid on silent auction items—this historic eighty-plus-year-old theater is entirely nonprofit.

501 Queens Rd., 704-376-3777
theatrecharlotte.org

GO ON A GALLERY CRAWL
AROUND SOUTH END

This bustling historic neighborhood just south of Uptown just keeps drawing galleries to its former textile mill spaces. Spots like boutique and gallery Lark & Key and artisan-focused shop the Boulevard at South End are popular shopping destinations in the creative hub. At the nearby DOMA Gallery, photography lovers can scope out contemporary shots, while at Ciel Gallery, you'll find breathtaking fine art mosaics. Gallery crawls on the first Friday of each month offer the opportunity to pop into more than a dozen of the spaces—and often catch local artists at work. Plan on ending your evening in an equally local manner at South End's nearby popular Food Truck Fridays, where the city's top trucks gather to offer their casual fare.

historicsouthend.com

CLICK A PIC
WITH *THE FIREBIRD*

The sparkly sculpture in front of the Bechtler Museum of Modern Art was only unveiled in 2009, but it's already one of the city's most iconic draws. Nicknamed the Disco Chicken, this mirrored mosaic of feathers by French-American artist Niki de Saint Phalle stands seventeen feet five inches and faces South Tryon Street. Pass by it and most days you're likely to find someone standing beneath its wide reflective wings for a photo with the beloved bird, which even has its own Twitter account and Facebook fan page. To top off any Charlotte scrapbook, snap your own shot with the playful piece.

420 S. Tryon St., 704-353-9200
bechtler.org

SHOPPING AND FASHION

HUNT FOR TREASURE
AT METROLINA TRADESHOW EXPO

From shabby chic décor to retro garb, a day spent browsing through this monthly antique market is sure to turn up fun finds. Located just north of town, this large expo features both indoor and outdoor exhibits and costs just $5 to enter. While it is open each month, the Spring Spectacular in April and the Fall Extravaganza in November feature the most vendors and are your best bets for top finds. Inside, bargain hunters can dig through bins of magazines from the 1950s, wander through shelves of fine cut glass, and push through racks of vintage dresses and jewels. With vendors from around the country, you'll find a variety of eccentric inventory here unlike anywhere else in town. Plan on enjoying a lunch break from shopping. Local barbecue and hot apple pies are perfect for enjoying at the outdoor picnic tables while you think about which treasures you want to take home.

7100 Statesville Rd., 704-596-4650
metrolinatradeshowexpo.com

PERUSE AND PICK
AT SLEEPY POET ANTIQUE MALL

For bargain hunters and vintage lovers, there's no better spot than Sleepy Poet to spend a rainy Saturday. The fifty-five-thousand-square-foot antique mall features more than 250 booths offering décor, clothing, furniture, and more. Wandering its aisles feels like a virtual treasure hunt as you stumble across a pile of rare books, a vintage typewriter, or a silver teapot just in need of a good polish. Plan on staying a while, as you'll want to explore every corner. Head toward the back, where a booth sells old records, while the one across the aisle is the perfect spot to pick up a *Mad Men*–style frock. While most of the vendors aren't in their booths, if you have questions about the items or prefer to ask for a lower price, the friendly staff is happy to contact them for you.

sleepypoetstuff.com

TIP

Brave the crowds and go on Saturday when Papi Queso and Cupcake Delirium food trucks pull up in the parking lot. The Little Green Muenster, a grilled cheese stuffed with muenster, avocado, spinach, and wasabi horseradish sauce, is the perfect mid-shopping break.

BARGAIN HUNT
ON EAST BOULEVARD

For one Saturday each spring, more than a dozen shops and businesses in the central retail area of the Dilworth neighborhood join together to offer up some of the city's best deals at their annual sidewalk sale. Such upscale women's boutiques as Sloane, Petal, and Coral line the street with their designer duds at seriously discounted prices. The sale was originally launched by the charming Cottage Chic shop, which continues to be a favorite with its grassy front yard filled with marked-down linens, soaps, candles, clothes, and jewelry. While participating stores don't typically announce their respective sales until shortly before the event, this is one day the city's savviest shoppers anticipate year-round.

East Boulevard, Dilworth

While You're There

Visit gift, book, and stationery store Paper Skyscraper. This tastefully curated shop constantly receives accolades for its gorgeous selection of, well, everything. You'll find fragrant candles and soaps, modern home décor, amusing cards and magnets, and one of the best book selections in town. Also keep an eye out for its annual summer sale, which offers the chance to grab some of the gorgeous goods at seriously discounted prices.

330 East Blvd., 704-333-7130
paperskyscraper.com

SHOP 'TIL YOU DROP
AT SOUTHPARK MALL

From browsing fashionistas to fast buyers, this sophisticated mall in Charlotte's tree-filled SouthPark neighborhood is a favorite for all shopping types. At more than 1.5 million square feet, it's the largest shopping mall in the Carolinas; but forget quantity, this avant-garde mall offers an impressively well-curated selection of luxe shops. Neiman Marcus, Louis Vuitton, Apple, Burberry, Tiffany & Co., Kate Spade, and Tory Burch are just a few of the more affluent stores lining its upscale halls. Ready for a break from retail? Rest your feet and feel refreshed in one of the mall's many bright atriums. Or, if you're spending the day, plan on lunch at the popular Cowfish Sushi Burger Bar adjacent to the mall, which offers sushi, burgers, and its famed mix of the two: burgushi.

4400 Sharon Rd., 704-364-4411
simon.com/mall/southpark

SUGGESTED ITINERARIES
FOR THE FOODIES

OUTDOOR ADVENTURE

FAMILY FUN

• •

HITS FOR MUSIC LOVERS

• •

DRINK UP

IT'S A DATE

• •

SPORTY SPOTS

SHOP AROUND

ART SMART

ONLY IN CHARLOTTE

• •

ACTIVITIES
BY SEASON

Of course, there are always spots to have fun around Charlotte, but a few of these activities will be best enjoyed—or only enjoyed—at certain times of year. Here are some suggestions for scheduling your fun by season.

WINTER

Warm Up at Lupie's Café, 25
Watch the Leonard Bearstein Symphony in Founders Hall, 40
Ring in the New Year in Center City, 41
Hit the Clubs for CIAA, 44
Take a Twirl on Uptown's Ice Rink, 60
Back the Buzz at a Hornets Game, 72
Line Up for the Lights in McAdenville, 90
Catch a Carriage Around Uptown, 103

SPRING

SUMMER

• •

FALL

• •

INDEX

● ●

• •

● ●